MEMOIRS

OF

THE REVEREND

k

William Huntington, S.S.

THE

Coal-Heaver,

LATE MINISTER OF PROVIDENCE CHAPEL,

GRAY'S INN LANE,

INTERSPERSED WITH

VARIOUS ANECDOTES FROM HIS WRITINGS.

SECOND EDITION,

REVISED AND IMPROVED BY ONE OF HIS CONGREGATION.

London:

MEMOIRS

OF THE LATE

REV. WILLIAM HUNTINGTON, S.S.

———

GOD has condescended to make use of various means for bringing men to the light of his everlasting Gospel, and many very humble instruments to the furtherance of his almighty purpose in the salvation of men by Jesus Christ. The following text of Scripture is fully exemplified in the present Memoirs: 'I have chosen the foolish things of this world to confound the wise.'

WILLIAM HUNTINGTON, S. S. (whose family name was originally Hunt, but changed to Huntington from the circumstance of having an illegitimate child sworn to him), was born in the Weald of Kent, about the year 1753. His parentage must have been miserably abject, since, says he, " I was very fond of feeding my little ones, when I had wherewithal to feed them; because I knew how much I had suffered when young, through my parents' poverty." Another of his disadvantages he attributes to his birth-place. " Being," he adds, " none of the most polite parts of the world, I retained a good deal of my provincial dialect; and many of my expressions, to the ears of a grammarian, sounded very harsh and uncouth."—" When I was about seven years of age," says Mr. H. " my friends put me to school to an old man and woman, whose names were Boyce, where I learned my alphabet, and learned to spell a little in a primer, and so on to spelling in the New Testament, and at last to read a little. And here I remember to have heard my mistress reprove me for something wrong, and told me that God Almighty took notice of children's sins. This stuck to my conscience a great while; and who this God Almighty could be, I could not conjecture; and how he could know my sins without asking my mother, I could not conceive. At that time there was a person named Godfrey, an exciseman, in the town, a man of a stern and hard-favoured countenance, whom I took notice of for having a stick covered with figures, and an ink-bottle hanging at the button-hole of his coat; I imagined that man to be employed by God Almighty to take notice, and keep an account of children's sins; and once I got into the market-house, and watched him very narrowly, and I found he was always in a hurry, by his walking so fast; and I thought he had need to hurry, for he must have a deal to do to find out all the sins of children. I watched him out of one shop into another, all about the town; and from that time I eyed him as a most formidable being, and the greatest enemy I had in all the world, and would shun him if possible; but, if he happened to meet me unawares in turning a corner, you might have struck me down with a feather; I hung down my head, bowed and scraped, till I could get out of his sight, and then I fled, when none but conscience pursued. This man was a terror to me a long time, and has caused me to say many prayers.

"Punishment for sin I found was to be inflicted after death; therefore I hated the church-yard more than all the ground in the parish; and it was a rare thing to catch me there in the dark.—I would travel any distance round about rather than drag my guilty conscience over that enchanted spot.

"My friends not being able to pay for my schooling, I was taken away from school, and sent daily into the woods to fetch bundles of fuel to burn in the winter, and in the summer I went with my mother and sisters to gleaning, so that I soon forgot what I had learned before.

"I also remember to have once heard a person say, that all things were possible with God; which words I secretly treasured up, and pondered in my heart."

These sentences, which open his Bank of Faith, not only exhibit the origination of Huntington's religious impressions, but also his particular views respecting faith, which, even at this early period, specially included temporal blessings: for, says he, "as I had great desire at that time to live in the capacity of an errand-boy with a certain gentleman in the place (being very poorly brought up, and knowing much the want of the common necessaries of life), it came into my mind, that, if all things were possible with God, it was possible for him to send me to live as a servant-boy with 'Squire Cook, though, at the same time, he had a boy who I believe was well approved of." His idea of faith was eventually strengthened by his obtaining the place, contrary to all probability; and though, after this event, he "was still pursued with deistical principles—that God took "no notice of our proceedings," yet, upon the recovery of his eldest surviving daughter from an almost hopeless state of illness, some few years after, in answer to his prayers, he was " effectually convinced that all things were possible with God."

After various menial services, and "having wandered about some years in this solitary way, seeking rest and finding none," although favoured with providential supports, from time to time, in the midst of pleasure pursued in order to stifle the sense of them, Mr. Huntington married; and took ready-furnished lodgings, at Mortlake, in Surrey. Here " it so happened," says Mr. H. " that I fell lame, having received a wrench in my loins, which rendered me incapable of labour for many days. During this time, our money was all gone; and we were strangers in the place, having been in it but about half a year. After I began to recover a little, there fell a deep snow on the ground, which prevented me working for many days. Here Providence suffered us to know what it was to want. We had one child, about five or six months old, which was our first-born. It happened one morning early, that my wife asked me for the tinder-box, seemingly in a great fright, crying out—' I wonder the poor child has not waked all night.' She then lighted the candle, and took up the child; and behold it was dead, and as black as a coal! Here Providence, nevertheless, appeared again; for, about three or four months before this happened, a gentleman, in whose garden I at times had wrought, desired me to look after his horse in the country, while he was in town, for which I was to have one shilling per week. The very day on which the child died, this gentleman came down from London, and I got my money of him, for looking after the horse, which just served to bury the poor infant. My lameness, poverty, distress of mind, sufferings of my wife, loss of my child, sense of God's wrath, were the most complicated distresses I had ever felt. From this time, spiritual convictions began to plough so deep in my heart as to make way for the word of eternal life; which, at length, brought me experimentally to know ' the only true God, and Jesus Christ, whom he hath sent."

His fare was yet hard. For some years before his marriage, all his personal effects, we are informed by him, used to be carried in his hand, or over his shoulder, in one or two handkerchiefs; and even after he married, for some few years, he used to carry all his goods upon his shoulders, in a large sack. "My dame and I," says Mr. Huntington, recording these things, "now kept a house at a very cheap rate—two shillings and sixpence per week carried us through tolerably well. We soon saved upwards of twenty shillings, with which, on the Saturday night, I set off to Kingston (he now lived at Ewell) upon Thames, to get some of my clothes out of pawn, leaving money in the hands of my dame to get half a bushel of barley. It so happened that the apparel which I went to redeem came to so much, with the interest, that I had not any money left to bring home. This was a great trial to us; because our poor little girl (his eldest living one), who had been but lately weaned, had nothing to carry her through the week but bare barley cakes."

"I found that the small pittance of eleven shillings per week (as I paid two shillings and sixpence for a furnished place) would amount but slowly towards the getting my clothes out of pawn; whence it came into my mind to search the Bible, to see if any instruction for faith could be got about the matter. I turned promiscuously to these words: "There is a lad here, which hath five barley loaves with two fishes; but what are they among so many?' I asked my wife, if she had ever ate barley bread? she said, 'Yes, in Dorsetshire.' I told her I never had eaten it, but the poor Saviour, with his Apostles, had; and as God saw it necessary to keep us in a state of deep poverty, it ill became us to complain, or to refuse the meanest diet, seeing he had blessed us with an assured hope of heaven hereafter. She said, she was willing, if I was." What with working by day, and living upon barley, and cobbling at nights, though they kept out of debt and decent in clothes, our preacher incurred a violent humour in his eyes, and, for some months, was in danger of losing his sight.—But to return.

"Though we could eat barley, I could not endure to see our infant live on that only. On the Monday following, indeed, I went to work heavily, and very much distressed to know how my poor little one was to live. But as I went over a bridge, that led to my work, I cast my eye on the right-hand side, where lay a very large eel on the mud, by the river side, apparently dead: I caught hold of it, and soon found it was only asleep. My little one was very fond of it, and it richly supplied all her wants that day; but at night I was informed the eel was gone, so the next day afforded me the same distress as the preceding day had done. When thus going to my work, cruelly reflecting on myself for parting with all my money, just as I entered the garden gates, I saw a partridge lie dead on the walk. I took it up, and found it warm; so I carried it home, and a few days after this, my master told me he had found a partridge on he garden-walk also, but that it stunk: I told him I had found one a little before that time. He observed, that two males had been fighting, and had killed each other, which was very common. But I was enabled to look higher. Carnal reason always traces every thing from God to second causes, and there leaves them floating upon uncertainties; but faith traces up to their first cause, and fixes them there, by which means God's hand is known, and himself glorified. I believe, this battle between the plumed warriors was proclaimed by the Lord: for if a sparrow falls not to the ground without God's leave, as the Scriptures declare, I can hardly think a partridge does."

" During my residence at Ewell," subjoins the preacher, " I often begun the week with eighteen or twenty pence, sometimes with two shillings, and sometimes with half a crown; and we have lived through the week on that only, without contracting any debt; and I found it impossible at the week's end, upon the best reflection I could make, to tell how we had been supported through the week. At other times, I have found that my craving appetite had lost its keenness, insomuch that I have been able to work hard for two days together without any food at all. And, sometimes, God has indulged me with such heavenly views of a glorified state, and entertained my mind with such sweet contemplations on futurity, that my dinner hour has passed away unnoticed; nor have I once had a thought about it till four or five o'clock, or near the time of leaving my labour."

Ewell deserves our consideration on another account. It was at Ewell Marsh, whither he had come in his low estate: " When the cart set us down on Ewell Marsh (says he) on the Monday morning, and I had paid the hire of it, I had the total sum of ten-pence halfpenny left—to provide for myself, my wife, and child, till the ensuing Saturday night! But, though I was thus poor, I knew God had made me rich in faith; and these words came on my mind with power: ' He multiplied the loaves and fishes to feed five thousand men, besides women and children.' We went on our knees, and turned the account of that miracle into a prayer; beseeching the Almighty to multiply what we had, or to send relief another way, as his infinite wisdom thought most proper.

" The next evening my landlord's daughter and son-in-law came up to see their mother, with whom I now lodged; and brought some baked meat, which they had just taken out of their oven, for me and my wife to sup along with them. These poor people knew nothing of us nor of our God. The next day in the evening, they did the same : and kept sending victuals or garden-stuff to us all the week long. Some time after this God began to work upon the husband, and then I related the circumstance : at the hearing of which, he told me how it was impressed on his mind that I was in want of victuals; when his wife found fault with him for thinking so, and bringing it to me, saying, ' The people are better to pass than we are.' But he contradicted her, and insisted on her doing as he desired. It pleased God (adds Mr. H.) sorely to afflict this poor man, some few years after; during which time I was enabled to restore him four-fold. He left a testimony for God with his dying breath, and I believe he is in eternal glory." His name was Webb.

At Ewell Marsh also Mr. H. first entered on his public life. He was, nevertheless, still poor. Partly to remedy this evil, and partly to obtain something more nourishing than barley, his wife now proposed that she should go to gleaning; but the farmers drove her out of the fields, and the gleaners came about her, like a shoal of small birds attending the funeral of a dead hawk, swearing that parsons' wives should not glean there.—' What,' said they, ' wives of the clergy go a gleaning!' But his dame persevered in her work. " Notwithstanding their chasing the clergyman's wife from field to field, she gleaned as much or more than Ruth of old did; and, when harvest came on again, went to gleaning as before." Her husband's " continuing to preach," however, " had alarmed and much offended the whole parish : therefore they were more fierce in pursuing her. On the other hand, some were afraid of going near her lest they should catch a religious infection; it being reported abroad, that there was something of a power had seized upon them, and held them so fast that they must immediately change their own religion." So much did the superstitious imagination overpower vulgar minds, at the time, that men were accustomed to go quite out of their path, whenever they encountered our preacher, and take a circle in the field, rather than pass him on the road; as if that secret something could not seize them (observes Mr. Huntington) whilst walking on the grass, as well as on the footpath!

Persecution at length drove Mr. Huntington to Thames Ditton, where he was first compelled to embark in the servilely laborious occupation of coal-heaving. This appears to have been that precise portion of his existence during which he felt most disgust, and to which he never reverts without some expression of indignant grief.

Notwithstanding the spiritual manifestations he there experienced, during an illness at once dangerous and trying, yet the people of the place, contemning him on account of his employment, which ignorant men too naturally would, and rejecting his ministry, he appears to have considered Thames Ditton not a place where his preaching would be made useful.

It was while at Thames Ditton, indeed, that the Rev. William Huntington experienced those particular premonitions which evidently determined his course through life. "After preaching at Wooking, one evening," says he, "and having an infant very ill, I told my dame that I would lie alone that night, &c. Accordingly I went into another bed, and fell into a very sound sleep: when I dreamed, and, behold! in my dream I thought I heard the Lord call to me with a very shrill, distinct voice, saying.—'Son of man! son of man, prophesy; son of man! prophesy!' I answered—'Lord, what shall I prophesy?' The voice came again saying—'Prophesy upon the thick boughs.' I immediately awoke; and felt a comfortable power on my heart, and thought the voice seemed fresh in my ears. I got up immediately and traced my Bible, to see if I could find those words there; thinking that, if I could, I should conclude the dream to be from God. I soon found the words (Ezekiel, xxxi. 3, &c.), and perceived the thick boughs to be men; but what the command could mean, I could not then tell." Shortly after, however, says Mr. H. while ruminating upon the conduct of the people to him, "it was suddenly impressed on my mind to leave Thames Ditton, and take a house in London; that I should leave these little places in the country (he was ordained at Wooking just then), and preach in the great metropolis, where hearers were more numerous; and that this was the meaning of the words that came to me in the vision. Under this impulse I found myself very happy, and was thankful to God for my intended removal; it seemed, to me, so clearly to be of him."
After some consultation with friends, he accordingly took a

house, and fixed himself in London. Thus far his vision appeared true. The next thing he had to observe was, whether the boughs were thick or not? " I then believed," adds Mr. H. " that the other part of the vision would be fulfilled, though all the world should oppose it; and, having opened a larger chapel than I preached in at first, this seemed still to confirm it more and more."

" When I first began to open my mouth for the Lord," observes our preacher, " the master for whom I carried coals was rather displeased; at which I did not wonder, as he was an Armenian of the Armenians, or a Pharisee of the Pharisees. I told him, however, that I should prophesy unto thousands before I died; and soon after, the doors began to be opened to receive my message. When this appeared, and I had left the slavish employment of coal carrying, others objected to my master, against such a fellow as me taking up the office of a minister. His answer was— ' Let him alone; I once heard him say that he should prophesy to thousands before he died; let us see whether this prophecy comes to pass or not.' Many professors and possessors of grace opposed me, as well as did the world; some, from a principle of jealousy; others, from a principle of love, fearing I should run before I was sent; but they knew not the impulse I was under. In answer to my petitions, the Lord applied these words to my heart, and gave me a strong faith in them: ' A man's gift maketh room for him, and bringeth him before great men.' At length, I was led to see that I must be weaned from the church, as well as from the world."

His first priestlike livery was made out of an old black coat and waistcoat given him by some gentlemen who had invited him to preach at Mitcham; " my usual appearance (says Mr. H.) being more like the ploughman, or the fisherman. As it had been reported that a coal-heaver was coming to preach there, a great many people gathered together to hear me. After I had finished my discourse, a lady came to me, and gave me a new book, and blessed me; while a gentleman put a letter into my hand, enclosing a guinea and four shillings, with these words written—' Take this, as from the hand of the Lord, for the labourer is worthy of his hire.'—These kind providences of God did wonderfully endear the Lord to me, and brought me to live by the faith of him for the supply of all my wants."

His views respecting preaching are explicitly detailed

by him. Having been kept constantly dependant on Providence, he was satisfied of his never being intended " to be
a preacher to the rich;" nor had he any reason to suppose
that he was designed " for a preacher to please Pharisees,"
since he dared not place any confidence in the flesh, nor
even in the fruits of faith: but he believed that God intended he " should preach faith," having preserved him dependant by faith, both by spiritual and temporal supplies.
God, he was persuaded, had commissioned him to be " a minister to the ignorant," by sending him to preach, and giving
him many seals to his ministry, before he could read a chapter
in the Bible with propriety; and " to the poor," likewise,
" because he was sent without a penny in his pocket, and
because the many seals of his ministry consisted chiefly of
the poor, both in town and country." The vanity, therefore,
of worldly wisdom—the excellency of divine knowledge—
the uncertainty of worldly riches—the preciousness of faith's
wealth—the blessed religion of Jesus—the insufficiency of
human inventions—" all these" declared Mr. Huntington,
" seem to be some of the things belonging to the Gospel
which is committed to my trust."

Confidently as he had delivered himself to the poor of the
household of faith, Mr. Huntington with some difficulty
summoned up courage to preach in the metropolis. Con-
scious that he was destitute of learning, fearing that he
should not be able to acquit himself with any degree of
propriety, knowing nothing even of the grammar of his na-
tive tongue, and apprehensive of being exposed to the
scourging lash of every critic, we find that he laboured under much distress of mind for many weeks, on account of
his want of abilities. He preached first at Margaret-street
Chapel, near Cavendish-square, pursuant to advertisement;
where, notwithstanding his own mis-givings, one young
man was emancipated from a heinous error by the first discourse that he delivered, and afterwards became a preacher,
who " has been instrumental in calling others." Another
sphere was meantime opening for his exertions. Disgusted
with the errors that were intermediately broached in Margaret-street Chapel, Mr. Huntington, it seems, secretly desired to have a chapel of his own, though he felt almost
hopeless at seeing this wish brought about by one so mean
and poor as himself. " However," he observes, " God
sent a person, unknown to me, to look at a certain spot, who
afterwards took me to look at it; but I trembled at the

very thought of such an undertaking. Then God stirred up a wise man to offer to build the chapel, and to manage the work without fee or reward :—God drew the pattern on his imagination, while he was hearing me preach a sermon. I then took the ground; this person executed the plan; and the chapel sprung up like a mushroom."

Providence Chapel was thus speedily erected; and, though the name given to it offended many, " I have since seen," remarks the preacher, " a chapel called Trinity Chapel, where the Trinity is little known; but this was not the case at the naming of Providence Chapel." This chapel was in Little Titchfield-street, Oxford-market, but was destroyed by fire.—Mr. Huntington in his correspondence thus writes of this calamity :

" Such a stroke as this, twenty-seven years ago, would have caused our hope to give up the ghost; but, being a little stronger in the Lord, faith has heavier burdens laid on. The temple built by Solomon, and that built by Cyrus, were both burnt. The first book of Samuel and the 30th chapter came to my mind also, together with this promise— ' He shall not be afraid of evil tidings; his heart is fixed, trusting in the Lord.'

" It may cause a little rejoicing among the Philistines, as hath been the case often; they once triumphed gloriously when the ark of God was taken, supposing that Dagon had overcome the God of Israel; but their joy was but short— the fall of Dagon, the emrods, and the mice, made them glad to send it back again, and a trespass-offering with it ; for they cried, ' We are all destroyed, for his hand is heavy upon us, and upon Dagon our God!' This I know, that it shall work for our good; but how, I know not: if I did, I must walk by sight and not by faith. Bless God! we are not in beggary yet, nor ever shall."

" On the evening of July 13th, 1810," says Mr. Huntington, in his sermon at the opening of New Providence Chapel, in Gray's Inn-Lane, Sunday, the 23d of June, 1811, " a fire broke out at some distance from the chapel, when it was entirely burned to the ground. At this catastrophe, I am told, that two gentlemen, in particular, made themselves very merry, both of whose dwelling-houses have since shared the same fate! ' Man is born to trouble;' and it is plain that these good men have no more assurance of being exempted from calamity than we have. I was much surprised that, on hearing the circumstance, it did not in the least alarm or move me. But my mind was wonderfully supported; and, considering that it was not destroyed through any neglect or carelessness of mine, or any of the congregation, I believed that the hand of God was in it; that he gave it to us, and that he now took it away from us. ' Shall there be evil in the city, and the Lord hath not done it?' Amos, iii. 6. I had moreover a persuasion that, according to God's word, it would work together for good, but how I knew not. Sometimes I thought that my work in town might be finished, and it was intended to drive me into the country, to labour as an itinerant. And my mind was kept in suspense for some months about going into the country, till God stirred up the spirit of the people to build another chapel. And those whose hands laid the foundation of this house, their hands have also finished it, and have brought forth the topstone, with a repetition of the old inscription, ascribing it to Providence."

Both chapels owed their existence to the liberality of Mr. Huntington's congregation; who, when the latter was completed, generously assigned the legal property to Mr. H.

He also had a lecture on Tuesday evenings, at the celebrated Dr. Fordyce's meeting-house, Monkwell-street, for the convenience of the citizens.

Although not so rich as he was thought, he had for some years kept his carriage. " I had told the whole company that rose up against me," says Mr. Huntington, speaking of the congregational commotions which were excited by his opposition to the writings of Thomas Paine, " and told them publicly in the chapel, that so far from their being able to pull me down, they must not wonder to see me in my coach when old age came on; nor was the hand of God withdrawn till this came to pass." He was seldom mistaken in such predictions as related to himself.

Another fact is well known with respect to his second marriage: It may be recollected that the late respectable magistrate Alderman Skinner, who was Lord Mayor in 1795, married his daughter to Sir James Sanderson, who served the same office in 1793. This lady, after indulging in various opinions in matters of religion, was brought to the knowledge of the truth by the preaching of Mr. H. and, having lost her husband, and he his wife, were lately married by special licence; but she thought proper to retain her title, and not the name of her husband. She survives Mr. H.

who, by his first marriage, had thirteen children, though many of them died before him.

Old age now came on. Considering the privations of his early life, however, and the laborious nature of the occupations in which he was compelled to engage, his declining years were less burdensome than might reasonably have been anticipated. His decay was gradual; and his dismissal from this stage of being, long looked for, was attended with perfect composure of mind, and but little bodily pain.

Wednesday evening, June 9th, 1813, William Huntington preached his last sermon. His text was, Rev. iii. 3, from which he delivered " a most faithful discourse," and which, says the Rev. T. Burgess, who heard it, " contained a summary of all his ministry, as pointed and particular as if he considered it his last discourse to them : perhaps he might have some forebodings—for towards the close of his sermon, he beat his hand hard upon the cushion, with these words, ' I am clear from the blood of you all.'—' For my part, I have always been determined to keep nothing back from you, but to declare unto you the whole counsel of God; therefore I am clear from the blood of you all.'—Huntington's Final Exhortation.

" However, this is certain, if there were no forebodings in his mind, the good Spirit of God, that was upon him, knew it was his last; for though he seemed strong in the pulpit, when descending into the vestry, he complained of weakness."

Some time before he fell quite ill, ' sick unto death,' he was remarkably happy in his soul; the inward man was so renewed, day by day, that the greater part of his friends did not perceive his decay. When once he was taken ill, he seemed sensible that his work was done.

Upon his way to Tunbridge Wells, he intimated his conviction that he should never return home; adding, that he had begged of God, before he quitted it, that he never might. He said he believed his work was finished; that he had laboured hard for forty years, and been enabled constantly to declare the whole counsel of God !

Lady Saunderson, at one time expressing her concern on account of his bodily pain, he said—' I had worse once with a burning ague, and had not a bed to lay on, without an earthly comfort; and now I have every blessing in Providence to alleviate my sufferings !' His heart overflowed with the goodness of God, so that he lamented he could not find epithets sufficiently expressive to describe to others the sense he had of it. His own account exactly tallies with this.—" Reflecting this morning early," declares the preacher in one of his private letters, " of what I have been, and what God ever has been; what I have done against him, and what he has done for me; the many servants of sin and Satan that I have been a servant to, (and where they are all gone to now!) and the servant of servants is now come to; what I have in hand, and what in hope, I could sleep no longer, &c. &c. &c. Looking back upon past experiences in Providence and Grace, is reading that part of the Scriptures which is fulfilled and sealed up; and looking forward in faith and hope, is reading the other part yet to be accomplished in us, for to the heir of promise all must be fulfilled." He was frequently filled with self-abasement, contrition, and meekness.

The last days of his pilgrimage he enjoyed great calmness and quietude of soul, and conceived a most child-like spirit. He did not wish to see many friends; as there presence interrupted his meditations, which were peculiarly sweet to him. He said—' All lies straight before me; there are no *ifs* or *buts*; as sure of Heaven as if I was in it.' He enjoyed serenity of soul, and solid peace; but no rapturous frames.

On the evening before he died, he signified an ardent wish to sup with his family, and have some bread and cheese. He asked the usual blessing, returned thanks, and praying for his family, got up to go to bed; particularly and expressly saying—' This is the last time you will see me in this room.' It seems they saw his lips move during the night; and, putting their ear near his mouth, heard him say—' Bless his precious name!'

The next day (Thursday, the first of July) was his last. When they gave him, at one time, some water and other liquids, he said—' God bless you!' When he required more, he asked for it, and for the handkerchief to wipe his lips. Just before he expired, a heavy shower of rain fell; the window being open, he turned his head to listen to the rain, with the greatest composure; and shortly after he went off, without a struggle, into everlasting rest and peace!

His physician remarked, that he never beheld a more composed and happy countenance.

He had neglected to sign his will, by which omission his family are likely to be involved in all the disasters of law,

He was present to perform this duty, within two days of his decease, when he appeared reluctant about it, shifted the conversation, and evaded the act. His motives for this conduct are not clearly known. ' Whatsoever thy hand findeth to do, do it with all thy might; for there is no work nor device nor knowledge nor wisdom in the grave, whither thou goest.'

His remains have been interred at Jireh chapel, Lewes, notwithstanding that he formerly intended to have been buried in the neighbourhood of Petersham; where, many years ago, in conjunction with some particular friends, he purchased a spot of ground and erected a substantial tomb, hoping there to rest together in the dust—' till the archangel's trump should silence that of the Gospel, and proclaim an eternal jubilee to the covenant seed of the Son of God!' But this has not taken place, and his remains are now interred with his friend, the Rev. Mr. Jenkins, in a tomb in the chapel garden. A stone at the head of his present grave, displays the following epitaph, composed by himself some time since.—" Here lies THE COAL-HEAVER; who departed this life, July 1, 1813, in the 60th year of his age; beloved of his God, but abhorred of men. The omniscient Judge, at the Grand Assize, shall ratify and confirm this, to the confusion of many thousands; for England and its metropolis shall know, that there hath been a prophet among them! W. H. S. S."

There were some parts of Mr. H.'s character that deserve notice:—Anxious to please his heavenly " Master," rather than his earthly " Mistress," Mr. Huntington " endeavoured as much as possible to get his dame to live by faith"—a lesson which few of the sex have humility enough to learn, and which still fewer find patience enough to practise. If, however, he was not over-indulgent as a husband, but made a helpmate of her who was the partner of his life, this conduct might be owing less to his disposition than to his situation, which, particularly in the earlier stages of his existence, was such as to preclude him from extending to his wife the comforts and pleasures she would otherwise have enjoyed. He was an affectionate father, who at one period struggled hard to rear, with scanty means, a progeny not only numerous but unhealthy; and who looked upon the unnatural avoidance of such a charge, though common in modern times, as both dishonourable and detestable in the sight of God.

The following letter will give the reader a very favourable opinion of Mr. Huntington's matrimonial feelings towards his first wife.

To Mrs. H.

" *Gainsborough.*

" Dear partner in life, and in covenant love! Grace be with thee, and thy little troop.—I am at present very well in health; I have enjoyed more of the powerful presence of God than usual, the enjoyment of him has been sweet to my soul.

" I often take a solitary walk by the river Trent, and muse on the wonderful scheme of everlasting love, &c. &c.

" I do not enjoy my comfort alone; I call you and the little ones up with me to prayer, in my faith; and surely my desire is that you and your little ones may be saved! I keep close to my study, and commune alone with my own heart. I sit, from morning till night, in my own room; except when I eat my meals, or walk by my highly-favoured river, the Trent. Give my love to Ruth and Naomi; and all, if they can read this, &c. &c.

" Fare you well!—Grace be with thee and thine; from " Your affectionate husband in Christ,

" *W. H.*"

Charity was (strange though it may seem) his failing. " For three years together," declares Mr. Huntington, when narrating the condition of his finances on his settlement in London, " I lost ground; for Satan waylaid me in a path which I knew to be charity." When he quitted the trade of shoe-making, and, without any present resource, began to depend wholly on preaching, he gave his " kit of tools" to a poor cobbler who lived near him! Become more master of the purse, subsequently to his establishment in the metropolis, he was sometimes stripped of forty, and even of one hundred pounds, according to the state of his pocket, time after time, whenever his aid was solicited by any person whom he believed deserving of kindness. It forms the trait most excellent in his character, and ought to be proclaimed on the house-tops, whatever were his offences, that the experience of necessity, instead of steeling, had softened his heart, which was ever alive to the distresses of those around him; and which, more especially to those whom he supposed to be of the household of faith, prompted him to be benevolent even to an excess. While thought rich, therefore, he died poor, to what might have been expected.

He has described himself as being "abhorred of men." His temper was naturally warm; his behaviour, even to some of his friends, often capricious; and he was at no pains to conceal either what he thought or felt. His polemical asperity had likewise excited foes.

He was not indolent at his post. He studied for the duties of the pulpit, in which he was 'instant in season and out of season,' and, if success be any criterion of ability, not less eminently great. Preaching, however, was with him mere talking—his discourses were as story-telling. There was no labour in his art. His action was good, and his voice particularly pleasing; and, unlike our modern enthusiasts, he did not think that beating the cushion, and an unmeaning rant, was conducive to the truths which he preached.

Among the writings of Mr. Huntington, which are extremely numerous, the chief are—"The Bank of Faith—The Naked Bow of God—Arminian Skeleton—The Coalheaver's Confession—Advocates for Devils—Barber—Coalheaver's Cousin—Forty Stripes for Satan—Innocent Games for Babes of Grace—Music and Odours of Saints, &c." Also an uniform edition of his works in several volumes 8vo.

We shall give a few extracts from his ' Bank of Faith,' that our readers may form their own judgment of the rest.

The Stone-Mason's Wife.

" It came to pass one evening, that a person came to inform me that a woman, apparently near death, desired to see me. Upon visiting her, she told me that she had felt the spirit of power while I preached the sermon from the text in Habakkuk—'It had horns coming out of his hand, and there was a hiding of his power.'—' My husband (said she) is a stone-mason, and gone to Ireland to be the foreman to a very large builder there, and I am in time to go after him; but as my good man has left me, for a time, the Almighty has come in his room.'—She attended my ministry for about two years. I dearly loved her soul in the bowels of Christ, as I had begotten her, and sorely travailed for her."

Is the Boo all hoppe, Daddy?

" I was very fond of feeding my little ones, when I had wherewithal to feed them, because I knew how much I had suffered when young. When I used to shut the cupboard door, and gave them nothing but bread, my eldest daughter would look me in the face with much earnestness and solemnity, and ask me this important question :—' Is the boo all hoppe, daddy ?' which, by interpretation, signified—'Is the butter all gone, daddy?

The Leather Breeches.

" I was informed, a gentleman wanted to see me; accordingly I went, and was admitted to the gentleman and his spouse. He wept, and begged I would not be angry at what he was going to relate, which was that his wife had for a long time earnestly desired to make me a present of a pair of breeches, as she had observed that those I had on were almost worn out with kneeling so often at my private devotion, and that if I would accept of them, he wished to add to them a coat and waistcoat, but he was afraid I should be offended at his offer, and refuse it.—It is none but those who would fain go bare-breeched that would pretend to say that a good stout pair of leather breeches are not a good gift. The good couple both wept for joy upon my accepting the clothes."

In another place he says, " I often made very free in my prayers with my valuable Master for breeches: but he still kept me so amazingly poor that I could not get them at any rate.—At last I was determined to go to a friend of mine at Kingston, who is of that branch of business, to bespeak a pair, and to get him to trust me until my Master sent me money to pay him. I was that day going to London, fully determined to bespeak them as I rode through the town. However, when I passed the shop, I forgot it, for my mind was not then thinking on carnal things: but when I came to London, I called on Mr. Croucher, a shoemaker, in Shepherd's Market, who told me a parcel was left there for me, but what it was he knew not. I opened it, and behold there was a pair of leather breeches, and in the breeches was a note, the substance of which was as follows :

' Sir,

' Seeing your nakedness, I have sent you a pair of breeches, and hope they will fit. I beg your acceptance of them; and if they want any alteration, leave in a note what the alteration is, and I will call in a few days and alter them.   I. S.'

" And here I may notice the peculiar kindness of my Master to me, in ordering leather breeches for me, and not linen breeches, as was done of old for Aaron and his sons; for I wanted the breeches to ride in, and, if they had been of linen only, peradventure I should have been sorely galled. About that time twelvemonths, I got another pair of breeches in the same manner, without being measured for them."

The Ham.

" At another time, when Providence had been exercising my faith and patience till the cupboard was quite empty, in answer to a simple prayer He sent one of the largest hams that I ever saw."

The Riddle.

" After this the bountiful hand of my Lord seemed to be closed again for a long time; but just as the spirit of murmuring and complaining began to operate, there came a letter to me. I opened it, and found the following contents:

' *Dear Friend,*

' *I have sent you a hamper, and have directed it to be left for you at the old place. The first present is for your wife, which is two ends; the other is for your children, being a cow and her milk-maid attending her; the last article, according to my judgment, is a very useful thing for you, and for every Gospel minister. J. D.'*

" Here was a riddle, and it puzzled us not a little. My dame asked me, if my present was a Bible. I said no, I believed not. Then as to the cow and the maid, we could not make them out at all: and I saw my dame's mouth watering at the thought of the two ends. There was no end to guessing about these ends. When the hamper came, we all got round it, to see what was the substance of the riddle in the carcase of the lion: and, when it was opened, I found that my present was a bullock's tongue dried; my dame's two ends were two large pieces of bacon; and the children's present was a cheese with the print of a cow and milk-maid milking her on it. Such was the present, and this was the explanation of the riddle."

But our minister was not only a considerable prose writer; he ascended the heights of Parnassus, and held sweet converse with the " tuneful Nine;" in other words, he was a poet. His poetic works, which are akin to his prose, are entitled, " A Spiritual Sea Voyage—The Spiritual Birth—and, The Shunamite."

To sum up the character of Mr. Huntington is a difficult task, and demands more attention than a mere by-stander can exercise. Suffice to say, that he was zealous in the cause of truth; a faithful servant to his Lord and Master; and both his preaching and writings show his firm dependance on a crucified Saviour for a full remission of sins.— If it be objected, that Mr. H. from not having a classical education, was unfit for the pulpit, the same objection may be urged against many of our Lord's disciples, who were, for the most part, unlettered men. But God's ways are not our ways, and he makes use of many as instruments in his hand, to call men to the salvation which is in Christ Jesus. The same God that raised up Luther and Calvin (those shining lights at the time of the Reformation) raised up Mr. H. as a faithful minister of his Holy Gospel. He met with great opposition, and so has the Gospel in all ages. Men will oppose it, because it puts a restraint upon their wicked actions; and that minister who preaches the merits of Jesus Christ, and him crucified, is sure to meet with the greatest opposition. But the humble reliance of Mr. H. on the providence of God, and his indefatigable endeavours in the cause of truth, will gain him the respect and veneration of every true Christian.

That Mr. H. had errors, we are by no means disposed to deny; but we would ask, Who is the perfect man? The Scriptures say, ' There is none righteous, no not one.' And we may freely repeat, ' There he is, *let him that is without fault cast the first stone at him.*'

Poverty was favourable to his piety. It kept him dependant on the Father of Mercies, and led him to be grateful for what he thus obtained. He has been censured for ascribing too much to the interposition of divine bounty : but, surely, it is better to trace his hand in every thing, than not to perceive it in any thing ?

His conversion did not take place in the usual way. Though gradual, it was special ; since his faith came by inward feeling, teaching, and providential observation, and not by hearing. Hence he considered himself as one really instructed by God. "The good Lord," he observed, " is still with the Coal-Heaver ; and will favour them that cleave to himself in them that he sends." When at the point of death, he spoke of those who had cleaved to his ministry, and said God will bless them.

His pretensions will be found, to have been comparatively high. Unlike the preachers of latter times, " the tiptop ministers," as himself describes them, of our day, Hunting-on did not pop up all at once into notice, and assume the crown before he had born the cross; but was obliged to buckle on his armour, and show himself valiant in the pro-mulgation of the faith he professed. He was continually derided, abused, resisted, pelted while travelling, burned in effigy, and his life not seldom endangered, that he might be said to ' stand in jeopardy every hour.'

Enduring all things, he had to surmount the opposition of enemies, on the one hand; while, by his successful per-severence, he silenced those who would have dissuaded him, because " they knew not the impulse he was under." We find him compassing both these point. He conciliated friends; he confounded foes.

Mr. Huntington's belief may be considered from the fol lowing brief sketch:

Amidst an age inclining to latitudinarianism in matters o faith, even his adversaries have allowed him credit for as serting the distinguished doctrines of the Gospel. Thos who could not bring themselves to approve of his contro versial acrimony, have, nevertheless, admired his theologica truths, and given due honour to the zeal with which he s assiduously maintained the religion first delivered to the saints. Justice prompts us to remark, on this head, that he chiefly desired to have a chapel of his own, after he quitter the country, that he might be enabled more effectually to re sist and confute the heresies at that time promulgated in London. He was in doctrine faithful to the end. During the last discourse he was allotted to preach, he, with un-common stress, exhorted his congregation to remember how they had received and heard, and thus hold fast; 1st. " The doctrine of the glorious and incomprehensible Trinity, and Trinity in Unity; 2d. The Divinity and Eternal Godhead of Christ Jesus our blessed Saviour; 3d. God's Election be-fore time; 4th. Redemption by Christ Jesus, in time, from among men; 5th. That we are Accepted and Justified only by faith in the Righteousness of Christ Jesus; 6th. Rege-neration, by the Holy Spirit." These were those great truths which he considered as essential to eternal salvation.

Many good men have objected to the title of S. S. or Sin-ner Saved, being the motto that Mr. Huntington judged lawful to claim. 'Sinner Saved,' notwithstanding, merely implied, according to his own explanation, the knowledge of salvation by the forgiveness of sins; "and this," he adds, "is true wisdom."

The following Hymn of Dr. Watts may not be thought improper here:

Who shall the Lord's Elect condemn?
  'Tis God that justifies their souls;
And mercy, like a mighty stream,
  O'er all their sins divinely rolls.

Who shall adjudge the saints to hell?
  'Tis Christ that suffer'd in their stead;
And, the salvation to fulfil,
  Behold him rising from the dead.

He lives, he lives, and sits above,
  For ever interceding there:
Who shall divide us from his love,
  Or what should tempt us to despair?

Shall persecution, or distress,
Famine, or sword, or nakedness?
He that hath lov'd us bears us through,
And makes us more than conqu'rors too.

Faith hath an overcoming pow'r,
It triumphs in the dying hour;
Christ is our life, our joy, our hope,
We cannot sink with such a prop.

Nor all that men on earth can do,
Nor pow'rs on high, nor pow'rs below,
Shall cause his mercy to remove,
Or wean our hearts from Christ our love.

The following lines from the celebrated Dr. Young are here quoted, which for beauty and sublimity scarcely have an equal.

" You see the man, you see his hold on heav'n;
A death-bed's a detector of the heart.
Here real and apparent are the same;
Heav'n owns her friends, and points them out to man."
                                    YOUNG, *Night 2d.*

We shall close the account of this eccentric character with a few anecdotes which have lately come to hand—

Preaching one evening at the meeting-house in Rope-maker's Alley, Moorfields, formerly the Rev. Mr. Towle's, he thus closed his discourse: "And now, dearly beloved, you may return to your homes, and tell your families and friends, that you have been to hear a Coal-heaver preach."

At another time, preaching at the meeting-house in White's Row, Spitalfields, speaking of the character given of Nathanael by our Lord—'An Israelite indeed, in whom there is no guile'—"such a one," exclaimed Huntington, "is your preacher."

Mr. Terry, formerly a bookseller in Paternoster Row, published the effusions of his pen in rapid succession; and to the "Arminian Skeleton" he, being an engraver, prefixed a portrait of Mr. H. with a motto from Scripture—'The root of the matter is found in me,' Job, xix. 28; but the best likeness of him was lately published by his son, E. Huntington, Bookseller, High-street, St. Giles's.

Proposals have been issued for a bust by Gahagan; for which Mr. H. sat not long before his death. It has also been proposed to have a full-length figure of him in marble, at forty guineas each.

Mr. Huntington desired that no funeral sermon should be preached for him at his chapel; but this did not apply to others who might be disposed to show him that token of respect.—One was preached at Wisbeach; and another by the Rev. Mr. Fiest, of Little Providence Chapel, Baker's Court, Holborn.

The chapel built by Mr. Huntington's congregation, in Gray's Inn Lane, cost nine thousand pounds erecting.

An anecdote that has occurred since the death of Mr. H. is worthy of notice:

An arm chair, in which he usually sat when he composed his works, and which was intrinsically worth not more than fifty shillings, fetched sixty guineas at the sale of his effects.

[The quotations from the "Bank of Faith," are not intended as a disparagement of the work, but to excite the curiosity of those who may be disposed to read it.]

THE END.